Reality: Utterly Uninhibited & Unhinged

Suchana Das

BookLeaf Publishing

Presentation by *BookLeaf Publishing*

Web: www.bookleafpub.com

E-mail: info@bookleafpub.com

ISBN: 9789395756563

First edition 2022

DEDICATION

This book is dedicated to my son, my husband, and my family. You all are my greatest strength, my only weakness, and my whole world. My life revolves around you, and may it be this way forever.

ACKNOWLEDGEMENT

I want to thank BookLeaf Publishing for letting me participate in this challenge. It is an honour for me to be able to do what I love and retain a lifetime memory. I also want to thank my husband for his never-ending support when it came to writing these poems. I thank my son, for making me a better mother and a better human being every day. Lastly, I want to thank my parents and siblings, for their unconditional love, without whom I would not have the life I have today.

PREFACE

This book came into being because of a writing challenge that popped up on my social media. I have always loved writing stories and poems, so I thought I should try this challenge of writing 21 poems in 21 days. I was inspired by my own life events, as well as those of my loved ones. I just let the words flow and I poured them onto my keyboard when a topic came into mind, every day for 21 days. I hope you all will enjoy my musings.

What's Love?

What's love?
No, not the song playing in your head ("baby
don't hurt me…")
Isn't it one of those age-old questions?
That have multifaceted answers and variations?
Some say it's the work of neurotransmitters in
the brain,
Why then, does it lead to so much pain?

It's not always that love and pain go hand in
hand,
But more often than not, that's what it comes
down to.
To see your significant other, in the arms of
another,
To lose your soulmate, to a terrible twist of fate.
Why do we love those who hurt us and hurt
those who love us?
More questions keep arising from the main
question- what's love?

Why am I going down this pessimistic road?
We're here to talk about love, and its humble
abode.
Love isn't always necessarily romantic; it's there
between families and friends too.

A baby loves their parent and expresses it by
saying "Gaga goo-goo".
A parent loves their child by promising "I can
die for you".
So many lovey-dovey names come up, like
'honey-bear' and 'sweetie-poo'.

Again, I am going off topic,
Why is it so hard to answer what love is?
Don't we constantly feel it for something or
someone or the other?
Feeling love, feeling in love, loving a movie or a
snack, loving our organized kitchen rack.
But I will say this- love to me is that moment of
an indescribable sensation,
Trying to describe it with tingles going down my
spine, feeling all sorts of emotions.

When I look into his eyes, and see the calm
before the storm,
Then I see the storm itself, a combination of a
tornado, hurricane, even a typhoon.
Crazy how the depth of those big brown eyes
seems to be endless,
When the destruction of his storms consumes
me, and yet I want more,
His touch, his mischievous smile, even his loud
(but cute) snores.

Feeling his hand on my waist, the other grabbing
my hair at the back,
As he plants a kiss on my forehead, lifts my
chin, and stares into my soul, pupils black.
My breath becomes shallower, faster, heart skips
a beat,
This dance of love becomes a song, set on
repeat.

Writing this now, thinking what exactly is this
love?
How can a person make you feel so safe and
adored; is he an angel from above?
Can I please hold on to this feeling and never let
go?
How can this love be like the smell of earth after
it rains?
Like the view of sunrise and sunset above the
oceans,
Like the crescent moon coming out of dark
clouds on a clear night sky,
Please dear God, don't let this feeling ever just
pass me by.

What's love? Did I even manage to answer it?
Is it too basic to say that love is like a mix of
honey, lemon, and chili: kind of bittersweet?
Self-love, romantic love, materialistic love,
parental love, intimate love, passionate love,

Who can keep up with all these types of love?
Oh wait, we all do!
Lost love is still love, it just takes a different
form...
I thought it was maybe a figment of our
imagination,
But no, love is the most wonderful type of
devastation.

Yet, we crave this feeling again and again,
Even after heartbreaks, we try, again and again,
It's what love does to us I guess, again and
again,
Waking up to the same person, again and again,
Raising our kids day in and day out, again and
again,
Smiling throughout life's hardships, again and
again,
Helping each other through daily battles, again
and again,
Being there for our friends and family, again and
again,
Re-watching certain movies and shows out of
love, again and again,
Ordering that white chocolate brownie once in a
while, again and again,
Loving, being deeply in love, dying for love,
living for love, again and again and again…

It's All About The Money

It's all about the money, money, money,
Are you hearing Jessie J's song (Price tag) in
your head when you read that line?
Answer me this: Can you relate to this
statement? Is it really all about money?
What is money anyway? I thought it's just a
concept or a medium of payment exchange.
Is it access to resources? Massive wealth? Coins
and notes?

You know what's funny, funny, funny?
When we die, when our time comes, what
happens to all of our money?
Do the banks have vaults for each of us when we
go to deposit/withdraw money?
Why does money come and go? Can't it stay
forever and ever?
Why does money keep disappearing after every
paycheck like a magician's bunny, bunny,
bunny?
Why do some people have too much of it and
some have nothing?
These are the questions that plague me at night.

Is the amount of money we have determined by
external or internal factors?
Does all of our blood run differently? Is that
why money discrepancies exist?
Skin colour may be different but blood colour is
certainly not.
Then why are we obsessed with getting and
making more and more money?
We have like what, 70 years on average to spend
the money?
Or keep living in our own little poverty-filled
bubble with a lack of money?
Isn't this phenomenon of money quite sick? Like
a nose that's runny, runny, runny?
Am I asking oblivious questions that don't
belong in the 21st century?
I can hear some of you readers muttering "Yes"
under your breaths.

No, having money doesn't always make it
sunny, sunny, sunny,
No matter how wealthy you are, you can't buy
mother nature.
You can't eradicate poverty (I mean you can but
the 1% chooses not to).
You can't end world hunger (I mean you can but
again they choose not to).
You can't buy peace (I mean…even if you buy a
relaxing spa? An island for yourself?)

Nope never mind, you just can't buy peace or
sanctity, no matter what the currency.
Money, as they say, can't buy happiness,
Yet those who say that are usually those who
don't have money, how ironic!
Those who have a lot of money seem to be
doing just fine thank you,
In their luxurious, lavish lifestyles, evading
taxes, capitalizing on the lower/middle class.
Right up to the point of depression and suicide,
they look like they're doing swell!

Wait, so those who have less money are actually
less likely to be depressed or suicidal?
And this fact is backed up by scientific research
and data?
But… what…but that doesn't….where's the
sense in that?
The rich have nothing to worry about! No care
or stress in the world!
Why are they found with a noose around their
neck?
Is it like that song- "mo' money mo' problems?"
For the poor, should the song be- "I got 99
problems but money ain't one?"

Meh, I guess having money isn't always honey,
honey, honey.

Problems

Problems in life

Part one: The affluent and developed

My wi-fi is being so slow!!
#FirstWorldProblems
My pictures on social media aren't uploading
properly!! #FirstWorldProblems
I put too much milk in my cereal and now it's all
liquid-ish!! #FirstWorldProblems
The power outage caused me to miss a concert
and not have access to data on my phone, and
now I can't check who 'liked' my posts!!
#FirstWorldProblems
My iPhone is already one year old and I need the
new one ASAP!! #FirstWorldProblems
My camera quality is so bad in this new phone!!
#FirstWorldProblems
This filter makes me look fat and doesn't take
away my pimples!! #FirstWorldProblems
My car isn't going fast enough; it's so much
slower than newer models!!
#FirstWorldProblems
I just missed the bus; now I have to wait a few
minutes for the next one!! #FirstWorldProblems

We should all become vegan and have ONLY
organic foods no matter how much more
expensive they are!! #FirstWorldProblems
The colour of my cushion covers don't match
the living room wall!! #FirstWorldProblems
I only received a few hundred bucks in my tax
return!! #FirstWorldProblems
There were only 35 likes on my selfie, I must be
really ugly!! #FirstWorldProblems

Part two: The less developed and poorer

I have to feed my wife and children and I have
no income whatsoever; I have to resort to either
begging or stealing to feed my family!!
#ThirdWorldProblems
The electricity in the whole village is out for the
third time this week!! #ThirdWorldProblems
We don't have proper continuous access to
freshwater!! #ThirdWorldProblems
We have to walk many kilometers every day just
to go to educational facilities!!
#ThirdWorldProblems
There are no maintenance, hygienic, and safe
working conditions in these factories and
sweat-shops, even though we are the primary
suppliers of all the clothing/shoes brands in the
world!! #ThirdWorldProblems

The government is corrupt and the middle-class
is suffering, because we are sandwiched between
the poor (who are eligible to receive some sort
of aid), and the ultra-rich (who are not even
batting an eye at poverty-ridden communities)!!
#ThirdWorldProblems
The people on the roads and streets are not
complying with traffic laws, leading to accidents
and deaths every day!! #ThirdWorldProblems
The infrastructure of houses and manufacturing
warehouses are terribly weak, leading to
possible fires and other damages!!
#ThirdWorldProblems
That guy is walking barefoot because he can't
afford to buy shoes, and I am crawling to get
around because I have no feet!!
#ThirdWorldProblems
Domestic violence and abuse continues to be
ignored, seen but unnoticed intentionally, and
unreported!! #ThirdWorldProblems
Women in some regions are still not allowed to
get an education or go to work!!
#ThirdWorldProblems
There are no proper healthcare policies in place,
and random religious/political wars are
constantly breaking out, causing us to fear if we
will wake up to see the light of tomorrow or
not!! #ThirdWorldProblems

Drug use and misuse is a serious issue but there
is a lack of mental-health resources available to
help those who desperately need it!!
#ThirdWorldProblems

Who is to say which of these problems are more
or less serious? Who is the judge of the severity
of problems in life?
Next time you want to complain about
insignificant details,
Stop and think,
And perhaps be thankful for the life you are
living.
Someone out there has it worse than you...

Baby Talks

Baby thoughts

Right after being born:
"What is this? Milk? You gave me all the yummy foods for 10 months and now I'm stuck with milk?"
"Ooh boobies!"
"Why is everyone taking pictures of me? I literally just got here!"
Sigh "Life was better inside."
"Change me!! I am wet all over!"
"What is this pain in my stomach? Come on! Someone take this gas out of me! It hurts!"
"Yay boobies!"

Few weeks later:
"Why do these humans keep taking pictures and videos of all that I do?"
"Yay boobies!"
"Someone change my diaper!! There is a lot of poop in there and I stink!"
"Oh, you want to take a nap? Not on my watch!"
"Wake up and play with me! You had 2 hours of sleep which is enough!"
"Yay boobies!"

"You're tired of playing peek-a-boo? Too bad! I am extremely cute and I demand more peek-a-boo!"
"You know you can't get mad at me when I flash my heart-melting smile at you!"
"You want to use the washroom and take a shower? No way! You are going to sit here and play with me FOREVER!"
"Stop putting my feet in your mouth, it's highly unsanitary. Don't these humans know anything?"

Few months later:
"Oh look! Coco-melon! I love these cartoons so much!"
"Yay bottled milk!"
"Oh, you just cleaned up the house? Haha not for long!"
"Change me!! Don't you know it's my job to go through a lot of diapers every day?"
"Wow look at how many toys I have!"
"Nah, I would much rather touch everything else instead of playing with these toys, like the kitchen items!"
"Yes, I am crawling and sitting, why does all of this need to be documented on your phone?"
"Why is mommy and daddy posting my life on social media? Don't they know I want some privacy?"

"Yay more milk! I miss the boobies though!"
"Oh yes, please blow raspberries on my tummy,
it tickles! I like it!"

Few more months later:
"Ouch my teeth hurt! Wait I don't have any teeth
yet, why is my mouth hurting so much?"
"Need to bite on anything and everything! Give
me your arms to chew on!"
"Oh, look there is some dirt on the floor. Let me
put that in my mouth as well."
"Can I eat some solid food please mom? I miss
eating all those craving-foods when I was inside
you!"
"What is this mushy fruit stuff?? Where's the
sour and spicy stuff I had for 10 months?"
"At least I still get to keep drinking milk!"
"Why are these strangers taking me into their
arms? I don't know who you are!"
"What are these baby language talks they keep
saying to me? Speak to me like a normal person,
I promise I understand everything! I'm just
pretending not to so that you keep doing stuff for
me!"
"What is a sleep schedule? Never heard of it. I
want to continue ruining your sleep for a little
longer."

Few more and more months later:

"Why does mommy and daddy get upset when other babies achieve their milestones but I still haven't? I'm trying, I promise!"

"I have been on this planet for almost a year, and still didn't get much work done, hmm. What shall I do next? Maybe I should take my first steps and show everyone how much destruction I can cause in their house!"

"Ooh a TV remote! Definitely going to put that in my mouth, along with whatever else I can get my hands on!"

"I am liking these different foods my mommy and daddy are feeding me; keep the different tastes coming!"

"I miss mommy's boobies! And soon she is going back to work! How am I supposed to be without her for 8 hours a day?"

"You want to do a birthday party for me which has a specific theme? Bro, do you think I even know what a theme is? Will I remember this special 'theme' when I am older?"

"Okay I am going to start making some sounds and see if I can talk like mommy and daddy, so that they will finally understand me and my needs!"

Finding Silence

Listen to the silence they say, apparently it
speaks volumes.
But how can that be? Isn't the point of silence
'no talking'?
There is nothing in this silence, it's just…
silence…

Oh wait, I feel some kind of goosebumps and
nostalgia coming on.
This silence is making me ponder about my life,
my memories, my experiences.
Hmm, now I think I am liking the silence; it
seems quite peaceful.
It's like a slight escape from a mechanical,
robotic life.
Maybe I should close my eyes, and listen more
for the silence.

What is this feeling of serenity washing over
me?
Usually, I don't feel like this when I am at work,
Or when I am with my friends, partying,
watching TV,

And the street and traffic noises drown out my
thoughts,
Bills to pay, mouths to feed, ladder of success to
be climbed,
Competitions to be won for the survival of the
fittest,

No wonder it is so hard to find a moment of
peace and quiet in my daily life…

Why don't I make some more time for myself,
and just enjoy,
The Silence?

Motherhood

Motherhood

Part one

Doctor: "Congratulations, you're pregnant."
Heart skips a beat, slight flutter in the stomach, can't stop smiling
Thinks, "Should I tell everyone right now, or wait a while?"
Starts involuntarily putting hand over stomach in a protective way
Telepathically talks to the little embryo whenever possible
Deals with nausea, vomiting, fatigue, but smiles through it all
"I will announce my pregnancy to my dear loved ones, I am almost close to the end of my first trimester!"
Bleeds out suddenly while showering
Doctor: "I am sorry, you have had a miscarriage. You can try again."
Feels empty, cold, and dead inside. Just wants to go back in time. Make everything stop.

Part two

Doctor: "Congratulations, you're pregnant."
*Heart skips a beat, slight flutter in the stomach,
can't stop smiling*
Thinks, "Should I tell everyone right now, or
wait a while?"
*Starts involuntarily putting hand over stomach
in a protective way*
*Telepathically talks to the little embryo
whenever possible*
*Deals with nausea, vomiting, fatigue, but
smiles through it all*
Thinks, "I will announce my pregnancy to my
dear loved ones, I am almost close to the end of
my first trimester!"
"Oh! I have to start planning so much! Maternity
leave, baby clothes, a crib… what will happen in
my baby shower?"
"Oh, my goodness, I am growing a human inside
of me! In less than 9 months I will be pushing
out a person?!?! Or I will be cut open like a
piece of meat?"
"I am scared. I can't do this. I am tired. How am
I supposed to not work for almost a year?"
"Why are my feet getting so swollen? Why am I
craving foods that I never liked before?"
"Wow my baby shower was a success! I am glad
I am not doing a gender reveal, I want to keep it

a surprise! I will buy gender-neutral clothes and paint the nursery gender-neutral colours!"
"AHHH it's getting so hard to shave my legs or bend over to reach for anything! On the plus side, I am enjoying my daily walks!"
"Will I be a good mother?"
"I will definitely miss all this pampering and attention! What I won't miss is people constantly touching my belly even when it's unwanted."
"Oh my God, my water just broke. This is really happening. Okay, just breathe. You can do this. Women have been doing this for thousands of years. Our bodies are designed to take on this task."

Part three

Doctor: "I am sorry. You are infertile. We can try for surrogacy/IVF, or adoption."
Heart skips a beat, stomach drops to the floor, immediately panic sets in
Thinks, "What will people say when I can't give my family any children?"
Starts researching IVF processes, starts saving up money, looks into adoption agencies
Thinks, "But it's not my own baby if I adopt! Not my own flesh and blood! What if they turn

out to have serial killer genes and ends up killing
us all after 25 years of me raising them?"
"Oh, but there are so many orphans in this
world, it would definitely be nice and noble for
me to give at least one of them a good home."
"But what will everyone say about me being
barren? How can I look them in the eyes with
the child of another woman in my arms?"
"Oh, but those poor children in foster care would
greatly benefit from the love and affection of a
real family!"
"Will they whisper 'that's not her real child'
when we go out to places?"
"Why is the idea of adoption such a moral
dilemma in the current world? Especially in the
Eastern cultures or Eastern hemisphere?"
"What is the big deal with 'blood is thicker than
water' and 'having your OWN baby' instead of
giving a loving home and a bright future to a
child, who did not choose to be orphaned or
surrendered?"

Part four

Doctor: "I am sorry. You are infertile. We can try
for surrogacy/IVF, or adoption."
*Heart skips a beat, stomach drops to the floor,
immediately panic sets in*

Thinks, "What will people say when I can't give
my family any children?"
*Starts researching IVF processes, starts saving
up money, looks for surrogates*
Thinks, "What will people say if I end up having
a test-tube baby instead of doing it the
traditional way?"
"Yes, it's my own egg and my partner's sperm,
so the baby is still mine, but I am not the one
carrying it! Why should another woman carry
my baby in her womb?"
"Oh, but that surrogate will be giving me the
greatest gift of life! She will help us to bring our
child into this world, even though I cannot, due
to my physical conditions."
"Oh, I will not be a proper mother because
people will say that I did not go through the
labour and delivery journey, so I have no idea
what the pain of being a mother is; people will
say I have become a mother by taking a
short-cut!"
"But why should I care what people say? It's my
child at the end of the day, and another woman
has generously and graciously agreed to carry
our baby; isn't that the most beautiful thing a
person can do for another?"

Part five

Doctor: "Congratulations, you're pregnant."
Heart skips a beat, slight flutter in the stomach, can't stop smiling
Starts involuntarily putting hand over stomach in a protective way
Telepathically talks to the little embryo whenever possible
Deals with nausea, vomiting, fatigue, but smiles through it all
Husband/boyfriend/partner walks away, leaves mother alone
Thinks, "I have become a single mother. How can I do this all on my own?"
"How can I give my child a good future and a good life? My baby will grow up with no father-figure!"
"What will people say about me? They will point fingers at me and blame me for my partner leaving us. They will ask why I let him go, why didn't I do everything I can to make him stay?"
"How can a single mother feed her child, go to work, take care of her home, give the child a good education, and play the role of both parents with no help?"
"Should I start looking for a new partner to raise my child with me? But what if my child isn't comfortable with my new partner and wants their biological father instead?"

"Will my new partner resent my child? Will my
child resent me in the future for not hanging on
to their biological father?"
"How will I manage everything? Is it possible to
raise my child on my own?"

The answer to every scenario in all five parts
above is: Motherhood is beautiful in all cases,
whether it comes with adoption, surrogacy,
natural, or single-parent.
Motherhood can come in all shapes and sizes.
There is no one single way to become a mother.
You can be a mother without having the genetic
connection.
Losing a child (whether through abortion,
miscarriage, still-birth, illnesses, etc.) is the most
wicked punishment that one can go through.
Be kind.
You don't know their battle.

Women

They say each time a woman stands up for
herself, she stands up for all women everywhere.
But why have we let this patriarchal society
define and normalize this phenomenon?
Why is it that a woman *is usually expected* to
NOT stand up for herself, and the moment she
does, is the proud moment? What is with this
expectation of women being submissive human
beings?

Oh, you woman, you poor, misunderstood
creature.
Stereotypically portrayed as the gentle, tender,
fragile, caring, loving person, who has to have
the face of an angel, body of a model, perfect
body ratio of an hourglass figure, can cook like a
chef, earns a good income, loves their in-laws as
much as their own parents, has to give birth to
children and then go back to their pre-pregnancy
body, has to be perfect in every way possible,
well-educated but cannot (should not) talk back
to men, keeps the house clean and tidy 24x7,
always available for sex regardless of how she's
feeling, and much, much more…

Oh, you woman, you strong, courageous
creature.
You bring forth life, and yet, everyone forgets
about checking up on you once the baby comes.
It's even worse if you don't have a baby, then
you're pretty much useless, right? You cook and
clean and work for days on end, with hardly any
recognition or acknowledgement, because you
are expected to these things anyway (you're a
woman after all!), right? Why should someone
praise you for doing what "you are supposed to
do?" Why should someone say thank you for
making dinner, or ask about how your day was?
Who cares, right? It's just a part of who you are
"meant to be", right?

Oh, you woman, you beautiful, magnificent
piece of art.
No man can do what you can do. How you can
take on multiple roles with a smile on your face.
How you can transform a house into a home,
how you breathe life in any room you walk into,
how you become a superwoman in all avenues,
how you break down the walls and shatter all
boundaries like a goddess.
When the creator of the universe created you,
they put in the best of everything, including
unconditional love, and didn't put a limit to how
much you can accomplish.

You were designed with special care, my love.
Take care of yourself. You are not the fragile
damsel-in-distress that the patriarchy has
deemed you to be.
Not all superheroes wear capes and tight pants.
Only in fiction.
Reality has given us the gift of superheroes in
our mothers, sisters, daughters, best-friends- the
true pillars and literal creators of society and life
as we know it.

Earth

Will reading this make you think of the Earth
Song by Michael Jackson?
Do you shed a tear for Mother Nature when she
is begging us to take care of the planet?
Did you ever sit and think about how stunning
the world may have been before the industrial
revolution and human influence?
How lush the greenery may have been, how so
many species of animals may have wandered
these grounds, living in balanced harmony,
completing the food chain and circle of life?
How these oceans were unpolluted, how the
waters were untainted, and the creatures of the
deep may have streamed along, throughout the
seas without getting caught in plastic and other
junk?

Oh, my sweet planet Earth that I call home, I
weep and rage with tears as I sit here writing
this.
Thinking about how you gave me this magical
land to grow up on, how well-equipped you are
with the perfect amount of oxygen for me to
breathe, the perfect distance away from the sun,

the perfect moon for us to gaze upon at night,
the perfect fruits and vegetables and meats and
fresh water and building materials to sustain
society and raw materials to sustain life…

You are so perfect, my dear Earth, that you even
created the perfect level of diversity in the plant
and animal kingdoms.
You created some of the most enchanting
creatures, a lot of which we humans still don't
know about, and brought for us such
devastatingly creative natural phenomena,

How can a phenomenon be devastating and
creative, you ask?

Let's see how forest fires can destroy all in its
path, and yet, stimulate new growth by releasing
valuable nutrients in the forest floor…
Let's see how tsunamis can consume all in its
path, and yet, lift up nutrient-rich sediment in
estuaries and deltas, and disperse it inland,
thereby increasing the fertility of soil…
Let's see how earthquakes can obliterate all in
its path, and yet, influence the flow of
underground water/oil/natural gas, make mineral
resources available…

Let's see how volcanoes can annihilate all in its
path, and yet, create fertile soils, geothermal
energy to generate electricity...

Wow, mother Earth, you really thought of
everything!
You even told evolution to create the most
perfect masters of you- Human Beings...
We just happen to be so perfect, that we end up
killing you and many of your creations of
species instead...
We happen to misuse and abuse you, to the point
where we take advantage of your resources and
exploit them for money...
We just don't care about your natural offerings,
we would much rather be victims of capitalism,
and live our short lives arguing (and killing)
over money and greed...

It's you, my darling Earth, that is imperfect...
You trusted humans to take care of you, to plant
more trees, clean the oceans, save the species
that are threatened, endangered, or close to
extinction...
But no,
You made humans so damn smart, so
technologically advanced, so brilliant in terms of
coming up with new ideas and inventions,

To the point that I am using these inventions to write about you (i.e., my laptop, my Wi-Fi connection, and more)…
And still, there is not much I can do to help you…
We are sorry, Mother Nature; we have failed you when you need us the most.

Health is Wealth

Anyone in a sorry state of health,
Cannot accumulate wealth,
Because he can't work…
Health is riches!

Health is the most important and long-lasting
wealth,
But most of us are in a race to earn materialistic
wealth…
We can earn money if we lose it,
But we can't get back our good health easily if
we lose it due to carelessness…
Health is riches!

Health is the only wealth we are born with,
We even die with our health,
Health brings happiness and contentment to our
life,
Money cannot buy peace of mind, smiles, and
laughter…
Health is riches!

How can we enjoy the wealth we have gained by
working hard,

If we don't maintain a healthy way of life?
If we don't take care of our physical and mental
well-being?
Health is riches!

Avoid paying hefty medical bills,
Don't accrue hospital expenses,
Strive for good health,
Become less likely to seek medical attention,
You'll have more time and energy to work,
Be productive,
And you'll generate wealth…
Health is riches!

Even if you have too much financial wealth,
And all other advantages in life,
That life is not worth living if your health is
weak…
Health is the greatest asset for you…
Health is riches!

Animals

It is a common saying that we do not deserve
animals,
Because at times, they display emotions and
loyalty that humans just cannot compare to,
We cannot even fathom how much our pets love
us,
If only they could talk, they would sing songs
and write poems for their owners…
Yet, many animals are mistreated and uncared
for around the world,
Even though they would give their lives for us…

How can some people pour boiling water over
street animals?
All they wanted was some leftovers!
How can some people starve and beat their pets?
All they wanted was some love!
How can some people neglect their pets, or
inflict cruelty on random animals?
All they wanted was to live!

Aren't we the vicious animals then, by
definition?
Must all animals be subjected to extinction?

Hunting and eating and sacrificing these
glorious creatures for sport or ritualistic
purposes?
Where is our care and compassion when it
comes to animals?

Then again, kindness doesn't always come
easily…
An unfortunate thing really,
Even towards other human beings we act
wickedly…
How can animals be expected to be treated
differently?

Still, animals continue to worship us, provide
protection, guard our homes,
All they want in return is some food and shelter,
not be attacked with stones…
So clueless about their fates on the way to the
slaughterhouse…
Being offered up to an invisible creator of the
universe…

Accept my apology, dear animal kingdom, for
our misguided war on you innocent beings.

Love, Lovers, Loving, Loved

"Love begins at home", Mother Teresa said,
Yet, this concept seems to be nearly dead…
With the invention of smartphones and
technology,
Families no longer seem to talk to each other
properly…
Where have all the dinner-table conversations
gone?
Replaced by social media updates, phones being
used dusk to dawn…
Are date-nights for couples still continuing on?
Seems like Netflix-and-chill is the only thing
going on…

What ever happened to the good old-fashioned
walks in the park?
Holding hands, sneaking a peck on the cheek,
strolling around after dark?
What ever happened to movie nights?
Why do they now turn into petty fights?
Working like robots all day, repeat again the
next day,
How about a romantic evening on the beach,
come what may…

What ever happened to impressing one's crush
with Shakespeare's 18th sonnet?
"Shall I compare thee to a summer's day? Thou
art more lovely and more temperate…"
Gone are the days of sending each other
romantic songs,
But for those lovely moments, my heart always
longs…
Used to love waking up to good morning texts
and sweet messages,
Now those texts read: "Do we need bacon at
home or sausages?"

I suppose it is a part of growing up in adult life,
Date nights go out the door; it is pretty sad and
rife…
Would love to go back in time, to those random,
spontaneous midnight drives to Niagara Falls,
Instead, it's early to bed, and wake up to
work-from-home, dealing with customers'
calls…
Nonetheless, love is always there, quietly
beating from the heart,
The lack of date-nights and a busy life cannot
keep us apart…

Yes, after having kids, it's hard to even make
time for cuddling,

But here's the fact that has always been
befuddling…
Love continues to blossom and grow, like
well-watered plants,
Then how come lately the arguments turn into
rants?
Why harbour so much anger in the same heart
that holds love?
What's with the lack of mental peace nowadays?
Is it a sign from above?

Life is so hectic these days; can't even expect
more anyways,
Can't blame the partner for their stress; just hope
that it soon fades…
Hope that we can go back to being romantic and
spontaneous and crazy,
Because we only have one life, so can we spend
some more time together maybe?
Can we try to squeeze in some time for each
other, have some surprises?
Instead of staring at our social medias and other
technological devices?

Friendship

How do we even make friends? Why is it called 'making' friends?
We do not sculpt or build our friends like statues or Lego toys!
It's interesting that we say 'I made new friends today',
Well, did you make that friend out of wood and clay?
Isn't it better to just "BE" friends with someone?
Not 'make' them your friend?
Would love to hear one day "I love being friends with you"…

Do you remember your first friends in kindergarten?
How you played with them in the classroom,
Introduced yourselves, had lunch together,
Talked about homework and other topics together,
And then slowly you grew up, went to other schools,
Met more good friends, casual acquaintances, had some best friends,
How did this friendship form in the first place?

Is there a time-law on friendships?
"You must be friends for over 10 years for it to count".
Is there such a thing?
I always thought friends were those who look into the window of your soul,
And quietly understand your unspoken words,
Read your silent gestures,
And be there to lend a hand through all hardships,
That's what makes friendships,
At least in my eyes…

Those who do not judge your worst decisions in life,
But rather, sympathize, empathize, and give meaningful advice…
Those who love to see you succeed and climb the corporate ladder to the top,
Instead of being jealous, envious, praying that one day from the ladder you will drop…
Those who laugh with you, cry with you, break bread with you,
Love you, hug you, give their precious time to you…

"A friend in need, is a friend indeed".

Pursuit of HappYness

Happiness is the emotion that most people
attempt to reach, but fail…
Happiness is the greatest feeling felt from
within, which brings great satisfaction,
Maybe happiness is something that we can only
pursue,
Maybe we can actually never have it,
Kind of like the Will Smith movie…
Is happiness a choice? Yes, definitely.

Happy people do not seek happiness in people or
possessions;
Do you know why? Because of the way happy is
spelled, versus happiness…
Why is the 'Y' from happy replaced with an 'I'
in happiness?
Only due to English grammatical laws and rules
you say?
What if it's because the 'Y' stands for 'YOU'?
Think about it, if the 'Y' represents 'you', then
isn't it all about what makes YOU happy?

What really does make you happy?

Is it money? Freedom? Hobbies? Family?
Chocolates? Love? A warm meal? Shoes?
Clothes?
Have you ever stopped to think about the root of
your happiness?
When someone gives you a bunch of flowers, is
that happiness only temporary?
Just for a fleeting moment you feel appreciated,
And then does the happiness wither away?
Kind of similar to the fate of that flower
bouquet?

We are just in the PURSUIT of happiness in this
life?
Not actually GETTING the happiness itself?
Oh, but pursuit is defined as the chase, so then
we ARE chasing something that can never be
attained?
Or only attained for a limited time only and then
it gets replaced by other emotions?
Why was the world built this way?
Is it to balance out happiness with sadness, like
the light and dark, night and day?

To appreciate the happiness, we must go through
sadness,
Fair enough, makes sense,
But then why does the happiness eventually get
replaced?

It's because of our materialistic needs that are
never-ending
If we have a condo, we want a house,
If we have a house, we want a car,
If we have a car, we want two cars,
If we have two cars, we want a boat,
If we have a boat, we want a private yacht
And it goes on and on and on…

Why then, are we chasing happiness, if nothing
in the world can actually make us happy?
Or if having EVERYTHING in the world still
doesn't make us happy?
How can all the money in the world, literally
trillions of dollars, not make one happy?
How can people with all the resources and
wealth still be unhappy?
Because of sicknesses, illnesses, disorders that
don't discriminate between the rich and poor?
So ultimately, their happiness is taken away by
debilitating diseases?

What about those who have nothing to begin
with?
How do they claim their happiness?
They have no power, no proper food or water or
a warm bed to sleep on,
How do they manage to live life every day, with
the 'OFF' switch on their happiness?

Don't their lives matter? Don't they deserve to
live every day in peace and happiness?
Do they even have a choice to own a condo or a
house?
Do they even have proper shoes to walk with?
Or only a few pairs that are torn up?

Maybe happiness can be obtained, if we start
spelling it with a 'Y',
Not literally of course; it's grammatically
incorrect as we know,
But internally, if we seek out HAPPY-NESS,
maybe eventually we will be happy?
If we do what makes us smile, what creates
everlasting memories for us,
What brings over a wave of nostalgia and gives
us goosebumps,
If we practice self-care and self-love,
Will we then, finally, be happy?

Death

When you die, don't worry about what happens
to your body,
Because your relatives will do whatever is
needed to be done...
They will take off your clothes,
They will wash you,
They will dress you up,
They will take you out of the house and deliver
you to your new permanent address,

Similar to how it was when you were born,
Someone else gave you your name,
They gave you a bath,
They dressed you up,
They carried you from the hospital to your
home...
Funny how birth and death are celebrated almost
identically,
With the use of candles in both birthdays and
funerals...
Except that you blow out the candles with each
passing age,
But they light up the candles for you once you
are dead...

Many will come to your funeral to honour you
and your life,
Most of your precious things will be sold,
donated, or burned…
Your keys,
Your tools,
Your books,
Your CDs, DVDs, games,
Your collections,
Your clothes…

So why then, must we fight amongst ourselves,
About the most insignificant of things,
Worry about such petty matters,
Hold grudges and bare hatred in our minds and
hearts,
When we are only here for a short time together?
Aren't we all from the same brethren?
With the same journey in life and the same
ultimate destination,
Death?

And you can be sure that the world won't stop
and cry for you,
The economy will continue,
You will be replaced at work,
Someone with the same or even better abilities
than you will take your place,
Your property will switch to someone else's…

And people will talk about the small and big
things you have done in your life,
They will speak, judge, doubt, and criticize,

People who only knew your face will say "Oh,
poor thing!"
Your good friends will cry for a few hours or
several days,
But then they will laugh again…
Your pets will get used to their new owner,
Your pictures will hang on the wall for a while,
then they will be stored at the bottom of the
boxes…

Someone else will sit on your couch and eat on
it,
Deep pain in your home will last a week, two,
one month, two, one year, two…
Then you will join the memories and then your
story will end,
It will end among people, end here, end in this
world,
But your story begins in a new reality, in your
life after death,
Your life is earthly,
Where you couldn't take the things you had on
earth with you to the afterlife,
Those will lose the meaning they had…

So why then, must we fight amongst ourselves,
About the most insignificant of things,
Worry about such petty matters,
Hold grudges and bare hatred in our minds and
hearts,
When we are only here for a short time together?
Aren't we all from the same brethren?
With the same journey in life and the same
ultimate destination,
Death?

The beauty of your body,
Last name,
Property,
Loans,
Job position,
Bank account,

Your house,
Your car,
Academic degrees,
Classmates,
Trophies,
Friends, acquaintances,
Men, women,
Kids,
Family…

In your new life after death, you will only need
your soul,
The only property that will last forever is the
soul,
So, live your life fully and be happy while you
are here,
As St. Francis of Assisi said,
"Remember that when you leave this earth, you
can take with you nothing that you have
received—only what you have given: A full
heart enriched by honest service, love, sacrifice,
and courage"…

So why then, must we fight amongst ourselves,
About the most insignificant of things,
Worry about such petty matters,
Hold grudges and bare hatred in our minds and
hearts,
When we are only here for a short time together?
Aren't we all from the same brethren?
With the same journey in life and the same
ultimate destination,
Death?

Illusion of social media

Hello, my dear reader,
Nice to meet you!
Do you have a Facebook account?
Or maybe SnapChat, Instagram, Twitter,
Even TikTok?
Oh okay, you use one or more of these social
media platforms,
That's great! I'd love to connect with you on
these sites,
And get to see your pictures, videos, and know
more about your life…

I'd love to see your daily posts,
Where you look like you're the happiest person
on earth!
But wait, is that your exact real life?
I thought you just had a fight with your husband,
And a disagreement with your mother,
And you were disappointed with your child for a
small reason,
How come your selfie looks so cheerful?

Wow! 60+ likes! 100+ comments and
compliments!

That's a lot of praise and appreciation for that
selfie!
But didn't you use a filter to make your skin
look flawless?
These 'natural' 'no-filter' filters are trending
these days, eh?
They can make you look so good without even
trying!
But doesn't that distort the reality a bit?

Oh, wow, you are eating at expensive
restaurants!
Oh, my goodness, your home-cooked meals look
so delicious!
How can you afford all this lavish meals every
week?
I thought you were close to maxing out your
credit cards?
Ooh new outfits from online stores!
Wow are those home décor items in your
background from Amazon?
But I thought you were on a tight budget,
As you mentioned your financial crisis to me
when we met in person…

Damn! A brand new car!
Oh, and now I know your license plate number
too!

Wow I can completely see your entire house,
your family members,
The inside of your home, your belongings,
No privacy whatsoever huh?
Everything is posted right there on the internet,
Where it may stay uploaded forever,
Giving access to complete strangers and even
hackers…

Oh, nice, it's your birthday and you received a
ton of wishes!
Do these hundreds of people know your actual
birthday from memory?
Or are they just wishing you because it popped
up on their news feed?
Would they still wish you next year if you
removed your birthday from your profile?
Aww, what a sweet and heartwarming
anniversary post for your spouse,
Tell me, what special thing did you do for your
significant other, except for posting a picture and
a long paragraph?

Wow you must love your parents so much!
Such beautiful essays you have written for your
mom and dad on mother's day and father's day,
Such a pretty picture you have posted with your
parents,

Tell me, when was the last time you checked up on them?
On their health issues related to aging, on their wants, needs, cravings, plans…

Family

Family over everything, they all say,
Yet, how much do they value their family
anyway?

What happens to 'family' when mom is yelling
too much?
In your head you start resenting her and such…

What happens to 'family' when dad is at work
all night?
Will owning all his money when you're older
make everything all right?

Why is it so hard for us to obey instructions
from the family?
But when our friends advise us the same thing,
we listen gladly?

Do you realize the pain your family went
through to give you your current life?
Especially for immigrant families, where the
pain was equal to being stabbed with a knife…

Over and over again, your family worked all day
and night to provide for you,
In a foreign country where they could barely
speak the language, let alone be happy too…

Still, when you get a good degree and a job, it
makes it all worthwhile for them,
They can proudly smile and boast and brag to
others about their dear darling gem…

Yet, after you marry, you want to get your own
place and move away,
What about your family? Who will look after
them? Where will they stay?

After all that they've done for you, they'll end
up in a senior's home?
While you and your partner and kids travel to
Mexico, Barcelona, and Rome…

Then history will repeat itself, where you will
give your blood, sweat, and tears for your child,
But as Karma comes around, your child will also
forget all that you've done for them, which will
make you wild…

Then maybe you will realize the struggles of
your own parents and family,

Maybe then you will see the true value of your
loved ones and relations, finally…

I think this is why all the time my parents used
to say,
"When you become a parent, you will
understand only on that day…"

Love your family, unconditionally, it will be a
blessing,
After all, always remember, family over
everything…

Marriage

Isn't it strange how 50% of marriages are ending
in divorces?
Even 50 years ago these weren't the statistics; do
we all need to take marriage courses?
How can such a beautiful union of two people
end in a disaster?
Is it because the world and its advancements are
moving way faster?

Have you thought about the impact a divorce has
on your child?
How they feel like an outcast, and sometimes
lash out and act wild?
Weren't both of your souls connected when you
took your sacred vows?
When you exchanged rings, and became one
another's spouse?

Heterosexual marriage, homosexual marriage,
it's all about love at the end of the day,
When two people love each other, they will
make it work and do whatever is needed to
stay…
If somehow there is no way to achieve a
peaceful resolution,

Then I guess divorce is the only possible
solution…

I guess I am being naïve, but I wish this wasn't
the case,
I wish couples in love wouldn't just break up
over the colour of their pillowcase…
Yes, this is what's happening, or so I've heard,
Relationships ending over silly matters like
bedsheet colours; it's really quite absurd…

Why are there only a few marriages nowadays
that last for 50 or more years?
Not counting those that end due to deaths; those
bring me to tears…
How do you let go of someone who you once
thought was your soulmate?
Now you have to deal with custody battles and
upcoming court date?

How can such a beautiful union of two people
end in a disaster?
Is it because the world and its advancements are
moving way faster?

Universe

Carl Sagan once said, "The Cosmos is rich
beyond measure,"
Apparently, the total number of stars in the
universe is greater-
Than all the grains of sand on all the beaches of
our planet earth…
Think about this phenomenon for a second,
And let your mind expand,
Broaden the horizon of your perspectives,
On trivial matters of life,
And realize how insignificant we are,
On this pale blue dot in the universe that we call
home…

If the universe was a blank piece of white paper,
We, our planet earth, and life as we know it,
Would be such a tiny dot on that blank white
page,
Just barely visible as a speck…
Don't believe me? Please watch 'Pale Blue Dot',
A simple 3-minute YouTube video could change
all your perceptions…

Did you know, if we used a 24-hour clock to
measure,

From the beginning of the existence of the
universe,
To the creation of the Cosmos, galaxies, stars,
earth, other planets, celestial bodies,
Single-celled organisms, plants, land creatures,
Emerging forests, insects, dinosaurs,
The Ice Age, Stone Age, Iron Age…
These took up more than 23 hours and 58
minutes themselves…
Still, over 99% of all species that have ever
lived,
Are no longer with us…

And now,
The Modern Age, Contemporary Age, and more
of our current natural lives,
Our life as we know it,
Was only created at the last two minutes before
midnight in that 24-hour clock?
Which means our entire recorded history, on this
scale,
Is just basically a few seconds old…
A single human lifetime, barely an instant…
Think about it, really think about the greatness
that is your life,
And how lucky you are to be here in this
universe…

Our sun shines so bright that we need sunglasses
in the summer,
And yet, this sun is actually one of the smallest
stars in the whole universe,
And still, we are unable to directly stare at it for
long periods of time…
Don't believe me? Please Watch 'Star Size
Comparison',
A simple 5-minute YouTube video could change
all your perceptions…

Can you imagine the vastness of the universe?
Makes me want to bow down before all its
glory…
To attain any life in this universe is quite an
achievement…
Yet, we think we are the most dominant species,
Whereas we actually don't know what we are
doing,
We are learning as we go, creating, inventing,
innovating,
Causing extinctions of species on the way with
our human-activities and influences,
With no idea of how our present actions will
affect the future…

Still, we continue to bicker and quarrel,
About who is greater, who is wealthier, who is
more beautiful, who has more luxury cars,

Who has more mansions, whose body is more
fit, whose child has more awards…
The list of comparisons go on and on,
Not realizing that it is all too trivial in the grand
scale of the universe,
And life itself…
How these little spats should not be taken so
seriously,
As we are only here for a finite amount of time,
Then we will deteriorate,
And our atoms will join those floating around,
And we will become an ever-wandering figment
of the universe…

Note- The scientific sources used here are
from Bill Bryson, "A Short History of Nearly
Everything".

Religion

This is a sensitive topic, but I can't help but to
wonder,
Is religion for people? Or are people for
religion?
Can one exist without the other?
People need religion as a guidance,
But does a religion need people to be its
followers?
I guess it does, in order to be acknowledged as a
religion,
There must be a certain amount of devotees and
rituals…

So now, if all religions preach peace,
Why is it that the world is currently facing the
opposite of peace?
What's with all the violent streaks, forced
conversions, imposed beliefs?
Is it all strictly political?
Isn't it also a form of religious battle too?
Not everything can be blamed on politicians,
right?

What about those individuals who have taken it
up on themselves,

To raise their weapons and wage a war against
non-believers,
And 'defend' their religion?
Does the Almighty God, who is the most
powerful creator of the universe, really need
defending, especially from tiny humans?
Is God so fragile, that He needs EVERYONE to
believe in His existence?
Otherwise, He doesn't exist?

If God wanted a person to be of a particular
religion,
Wouldn't He just make it happen Himself?
Would He really just send some young-blooded
hot-headed human beings to forcefully convert
those 'non-believers'?

Does it matter if one person believes in the
'unseen, invisible power',
And another person would rather face towards
some sculpted statues?
And another person meditates, practices
chanting, and techniques of Zen?
And another person confesses and asks for
forgiveness for their sins?

Does it matter which Holy Book is more
'correct' than the other?

At the end of the day, shouldn't we all love and
respect one another?
If I decide to believe there is God in every
material and every living thing,
Why is that so upsetting to you?
Why do you need to push me to believe
something else?
Am I bothering you with which God is inside
my head, and which way I face during prayers?

If you believe that humans should live a certain
way, believe in specific rules,
Then why not just pass down those values to
your children?
Why do your rules need to be applied to
everyone else too?
Why do entire countries become divided up into
religious majority and minority?

I really wish I could find the answers to these
questions,
It would really help me to understand the news,
when there is a next time, I see vandalism and
brutal attacks on different places of worship,
Don't worry, there will definitely be a next time
for sure,
Terror in the name of religion has only just
begun,

And until people see that we are all one, that we come from one,
The bloodshed will continue to paint the rivers red…

Beauty and intelligence

Have you ever heard of the terms 'Sapiophile' or
'Sapiosexual'?
It means someone whose romantic (or sexual)
attraction to others is based on intelligence…
In other words, brains over beauty!
Beauty may be dangerous, but intelligence is
lethal…
Some say it is a flawed concept,
But is it, really?

Looks fade away over time,
Aging comes and takes away that flawless skin,
And replaces it with sagging flesh,
The pearl-white smile is replaced by missing
teeth,
Bones aching, weaker muscles…

But intelligence?
All the accumulated knowledge and experience
of a lifetime?
That cognitive intellect, extensive vocabularies,
depths of words…
Those seem to last forever…
Maybe that's why they say, "Don't marry for
looks"…

Sense of humour, the ability to have a scholarly discussion,
Passion for collecting books and travels; an open-minded soul,
Isn't it much more attractive than a person's physique?
Ultimately, we are all just pounds of flesh,
We briefly inhabit these slabs of bodies like a motel room,
Check in, stay a while, then check out…

Your inner beauty and intelligence can make you succeed,
External looks alone cannot excel in life…
Your brain undoubtedly has the stronger domination to rule the world,
In comparison to your outward outlook and beauty…

So stop trying to cosmetically or aesthetically modify your body,
And pick up a book instead,
Immerse yourself in a new world of stories…
Don't marry (or become) simply a good-looking ornament,
It won't last many years…
Build your personality, become spectacularly talented,

And that beautiful brain of yours will be your best friend, best asset, best resource…

Me, Myself, and I

When I was a kid, I was told to go to school.
Parents would say "Otherwise you will be a
fool",
First day of class, I cried so much;
When I went home, I smiled at my mother's
touch.
After a few days, I got used to the process;
Going to school every day was the key to
success.
Slowly, I began to enjoy my classes,
With friends I wouldn't notice how fast the time
passes.
In Bangladesh, from kindergarten to grade four,
I was looking forward to so much more.

But then I came to England, into a world of
hope,
With limited knowledge of English, I didn't
know how I would cope.
I began to practice with friends and family,
Then, I started to improve my fluency, finally!
Still, I kept reading and writing in Bengali
sometimes,
Because my mother-tongue is beautiful, like the
sound of windchimes.

After a year, I entered my high school life,
It was different, interesting, and my schedule
was rife.

At the same time, I began to learn how to sing
and dance,
I thanked God for giving me this chance.
Life was getting busy, so many things were
overflowing,
But I loved every moment of it, so I kept on
going.
Eventually, I was reaching the end,
Had no idea what God was going to send.
One day, it turned out to be a simple surprise,
"We're moving to Canada", my mom said with
cheerful eyes.
"Oh no!" I thought, "How will I manage this
transition?"
But I suppose everything has a beginning and a
conclusion.
My Bengali-British adventure had to end there,
"Don't stress", my dad said, "Life isn't always
fair".
Now I have to add 'Canadian' to the list,
Who would have thought my life would have
such a twist?

I began high school in Toronto all over again,
Due to my age, I was put in grade ten.

I became a popular girl in school, with a cool
British accent,
Living a fun-filled happy life, no need to worry
about rent.
After three years, I was accepted into the
University of Toronto,
Days were flying by very fast, pronto!
Neuroscience was my major for my Bachelor's
degree,
After four years when I graduated, I thought
"I'm free!"
However, I knew the importance of education,
Therefore, I did not take any sort of vacation.
Instead, I enrolled into the same university again
to do a Master's for myself,
Looking for research placements everywhere, be
it York, Humber, or Guelph.

I realize now, how hard the journey has been,
Now I know what achieving higher level
diplomas mean.
I still continue to participate in cultural
activities,
Through the beauty of dance, I can light up the
festivities.
I am so thankful to God for all that I have
overcome,
It wouldn't have been possible without my dad
and my mom.

Thanks to my experience, I understand the
difference in education levels,
It's like having to move mountains, not merely
throwing pebbles.
Doing research work has taught me a lot,
I want to keep learning and growing like a
flower in a pot.
I also tutor some children in my own
neighbourhood,
Helping and watching them learn and succeed is
what makes me feel good.
I want to encourage and inspire the young
generation today,
To never give up their hopes or dreams, because
everything will be okay.

If you put your mind to something, whether it is
school, arts, or sports,
You will attain your goal, and even be able to
rule the courts!
Keep striving for a better future, keep working
hard,
It will all be worth it in the end; you will not be
barred.
At the same time, take part in your culture, stay
true to your heritage,
You will see how great that will be for your
personal image.

Don't stop learning, be wiser every day than the
day before,
Education will lead the way for you, because the
world is yours to explore.